THE RAVEN
AND OTHER POEMS

THE RAVEN
AND OTHER POEMS

EDGAR ALLAN POE

Selected and Introduced
by Richard Kopley

SCHOLASTIC INC.
New York Toronto London Auckland Sydney

ISBN 0-590-45260-6

12   7/9

Printed in the U.S.A.   01

First Scholastic printing, August 1992

CONTENTS

INTRODUCTION
TO THE POEMS

James Barhyte long remembered that, when he was eleven years old, in 1843, he'd met Edgar Allan Poe pacing back and forth in a clearing by a pond. The poet had been reciting a poem with the refrain "Nevermore!"

Martha Susannah Brennan long remembered that, when she was ten years old, in 1844, she'd watched Poe revising this poem in her family's farmhouse, where he was staying. She recalled trying to help him by picking up and arranging the manuscript pages that he'd let fall.

This boy and girl had watched Poe compose a poem that readers of American literature have long remembered: "The Raven." First published in 1845, this poem was enormously popular in its time and has since been much anthologized, frequently taught, and extensively studied. It is a classic work of literature by one of America's greatest writers.

Edgar Poe was born to actors David and Eliza Arnold Poe in Boston, Massachusetts, on January 19, 1809. After his father's desertion and his mother's death in 1811, Edgar came to live with tobacco merchant John Allan and his wife Frances in Richmond, Virginia. In 1815, John Allan took his family to England, where Edgar *Allan* Poe attended boarding school. Returning with the Allans to Richmond in 1820, young Poe distinguished himself as an excellent student and athlete, and won early appreciation for his poetry. He also developed important new friendships: with his older brother Henry, who had been brought up in Baltimore; with Elmira Royster, who became his fiancée; and with Jane Stith Craig Stanard, who offered a maternal sympathy and inspired Poe's poem "To Helen." Mrs. Stanard's death in 1824 was a great loss for Poe.

Poe attended the University of Virginia from February through December 1826, excelling in languages, but his gambling debts led John Allan to withdraw him from the school. In Richmond, Poe found his engagement to Elmira Royster broken and his relationship with his foster father worsening; he voyaged to Boston in March 1827 and soon thereafter had his first book of poems published, *Tamerlane and Other Poems* (which included "Dreams" and "The Lake").

Poe enlisted in the U.S. Army, serving at Fort Independence in Boston Harbor, Fort Moultrie in South Carolina, and Fortress Monroe in Virginia, until discharged in April 1829. His foster mother Frances Allan had died, and John Allan wrote on his behalf for a commission to West Point. His second book, *Al Aaraaf, Tamerlane, and Minor*

Poems (which included "Sonnet — To Science") was soon published, and, in June 1830, Poe entered West Point. However, he became unhappy there and neglected his duties, thereby provoking his dismissal in March 1831. A third book, *Poems*, to which his fellow cadets had subscribed, appeared in April 1831; among the pieces collected were the autobiographical "Introduction," the memorial "To Helen," and the yearning "Israfel." Poe settled in Baltimore with relatives, including his aunt, Maria Clemm (David Poe's sister); her daughter Virginia; and his brother Henry, a young poet who was to die only months later.

Poe concentrated on his writing, working on both poetry and fiction, and he entered the short story contest of the Philadelphia *Saturday Courier*. None of his tales won the contest, but five were published in the newspaper in 1832. A work of his submitted to the Baltimore *Saturday Visiter*'s literary contest, "MS. Found in a Bottle," did, in fact, win the contest in the fiction category and was awarded the $50 prize. In March 1834, John Allan died, leaving Poe nothing. Fortunately, one of the judges of the *Saturday Visiter* contest took an interest in Poe. John Pendleton Kennedy tried to help Poe with the publication of his fiction; encouraged him to write for Richmond's new monthly magazine, the *Southern Literary Messenger*; and encouraged the magazine's owner, Thomas W. White, to hire Poe as an editor. Offered an editorial position, Poe journeyed to

Richmond in August 1835. He left Richmond a month later, apparently because of his drinking, but he returned in October 1835, accompanied by Maria Clemm and Virginia.

While editing the *Messenger*, Poe achieved considerable fame for his sometimes scathing reviews of mediocre writing, and the magazine's circulation increased notably. Also contributing to his growing reputation were his poems and tales — both original and reprinted work — appearing in the pages of the *Messenger*. In May 1836, Poe married his beautiful young cousin Virginia. At this time, he was planning his only novel, *The Narrative of Arthur Gordon Pym*, early chapters of which would appear in the *Messenger*. Poe's association with the magazine came to an end in January 1837 due, in all likelihood, to his drinking. Poe, Virginia, and Maria Clemm moved to New York City for a year, and then, in early 1838, relocated to Philadelphia.

During his six-year stay in Philadelphia, Poe published much. *Pym* appeared in July 1838, *Tales of the Grotesque and Arabesque* in December 1839, and *Prose Romances* in July 1843. Among the individual tales published in this period were such important works as "The Murders in the Rue Morgue" (the first modern detective story), "Eleonora" (a rich rendering of Poe's love for Virginia), "The Tell-Tale Heart" (a brilliant and influential psychological study), and "The Gold-Bug" (a very popular tale and another literary contest winner).

Also, in the later years of his Philadelphia period, Poe was, as we know, working on his poem "The Raven," which would exceed in popularity even "The Gold-Bug" — as Poe came to write, "The bird beat the bug all hollow."

Poe's editorial experience in Philadelphia was, however, somewhat disappointing. While the author served as assistant editor of *Burton's Gentleman's Magazine* beginning in May 1839, he was fired in May 1840, probably because of his efforts to start his own journal, the *Penn Magazine*. He served as an editor of *Graham's Magazine* beginning in March 1841, but he quit in April 1842 because of his great dissatisfaction with the periodical. His renewed efforts to found a literary journal, renamed the *Stylus*, were unsuccessful. Furthermore, the sorrow of his personal life was deepening — in January 1842, his wife Virginia began to cough up blood while she was singing. Afflicted with tuberculosis, then called "consumption," Virginia approached death and recovered, repeatedly.

Poe and Virginia moved to New York City in April 1844, joined shortly by Maria Clemm. He continued to write fiction, scoring an early success with the short story "The Balloon Hoax," and he worked as an assistant at the New York *Evening Mirror*. He revised "The Raven" — as Martha Susannah Brennan witnessed — and, on or shortly before February 1, 1845, the poem was published in the *American Review*, receiving great acclaim.

Poe frequently recited the poem — we are told that to hear him read the poem was "an event in one's life." He later wrote of his most celebrated work that the black bird represented memory — what he termed *"Mournful and Never-ending Remembrance."* Certainly an appreciation of the losses that Poe had endured in his life increases our understanding of that comment and of the poem itself.

With his new literary success, Poe soon became an editor of the *Broadway Journal*, where he published many reviews of others' work and many revised versions of his own. His volume *Tales* appeared in June 1845, and *The Raven and Other Poems* (a different collection from the present one) was published in November 1845. However, as Poe had noted in his poem "Israfel," ". . . this / Is a world of sweets and sours. . . ." Poe experienced at this time not only success, but also strong criticism, failure, and tragedy. In March 1845, his accusation of plagiarism against Henry Wadsworth Longfellow prompted a response showing how Poe might himself be accused of plagiarism. In October 1845, Poe's reading of his poem "Al Aaraaf" in Boston was badly received and aroused censure in the Boston newspapers. In January 1846, the *Broadway Journal*, of which Poe had become sole editor and owner, ceased publication because of financial problems and Poe's drinking. A scandal in literary circles followed, and then came personal attacks on Poe in New York papers (in response to Poe's own series, "The Literati of New York City"). These attacks led to Poe's bringing a lawsuit.

In late 1846 and early 1847, in their small cottage in Fordham, Poe and his wife and mother-in-law were in poverty, and Virginia lay dying. On January 30, 1847, Virginia died of tuberculosis. Poe expressed his grief in "Deep in Earth"; the poem "To M. L. S——" reveals his great gratitude to Mrs. Mary Louise Shew, who had tended his dying wife.

In the final years of his life, Poe was able still to produce substantial, enduring works of literature. It seems to have been partly in response to a suggestion that he write something "suitable for recitation" that Poe composed such memorable lyrics as the passionate and mysterious "Ulalume," the dramatic and symphonic "The Bells," and the lovely and moving "Annabel Lee." His powerful feeling for two women, Sarah Helen Whitman and Annie Richmond, yielded such fine poems as "To Helen [Whitman]" and "For Annie." And his sense of endless quest, what he referred to as "unceasing pursuit," called forth a simple and elegant poem, "Eldorado." Perhaps, too, Poe was treating "unceasing pursuit" in his 1848 book about the universe, *Eureka*, when he wrote of "struggles towards the original Unity."

During his last few months, Poe went back to Richmond, lectured successfully, and proposed to the widowed Elmira Royster [Shelton], the lost sweetheart of his youth. She accepted his proposal. Yet Poe was not happy about his imminent marriage. Leaving Richmond on September 27, 1849, sick, he traveled to Baltimore, where he again drank. On October 3, 1849, he was found in a tavern that was being used as a polling place; he was taken to Washington College Hospital. Poe died there, of *delirium tremens*, on October 7, 1849. His final words were, *"Lord help my poor Soul!"*

Even as James Barhyte and Martha Susannah Brennan always remembered their wonderful visions of Poe composing, so, too, did fourteen-year-old Charles William Hubner always remember his melancholy view of Poe's coffin:

> While on my way to art school, when about fourteen years old, I passed a hospital. A plain coffin was being taken to a hearse standing at the curb. Two gentlemen stood, with bared heads, while the attendants placed the casket into the hearse. With boyish curiosity, I asked of one of the men:
> "Please sir, who are they going to bury?"
> He replied: "My son, that is the body of a great poet, Edgar Allan Poe. You will learn all about him some day."

Richard Kopley
The Pennsylvania State University
DuBois Campus

8

THE POEMS

DREAMS

Oh! that my young life were a lasting dream!
My spirit not awak'ning till the beam
Of an Eternity should bring the morrow:
Yes! tho' that long dream were of hopeless
    sorrow,
'Twere better than the dull reality
Of waking life to him whose heart shall be,
And hath been ever, on the chilly earth,
A chaos of deep passion from his birth!

But should it be — that dream eternally
Continuing — as dreams have been to me
In my young boyhood — should it thus be given,
'Twere folly still to hope for higher Heaven!
For I have revell'd, when the sun was bright
In the summer sky; in dreamy fields of light,
And left unheedingly my very heart
In climes of mine imagining — apart
From mine own home, with beings that have
    been
Of mine own thought — what more could I have
    seen?

"Twas once and *only* once and the wild hour
From my remembrance shall not pass — some
    power
Or spell had bound me — 'twas the chilly wind
Came o'er me in the night and left behind

Its image on my spirit, or the moon
Shone on my slumbers in her lofty noon
Too coldly — or the stars — howe'er it was
That dream was as that night wind — let it
    pass.

I have been happy — tho' but in a dream.
I have been happy — and I love the theme —
Dreams! in their vivid colouring of life —
As in that fleeting, shadowy, misty strife
Of semblance with reality which brings
To the delirious eye more lovely things
Of Paradise and Love — and all our own!
Than young Hope in his sunniest hour hath
    known.

[1827–1828]

THE LAKE

In youth's spring, it was my lot
To haunt of the wide earth a spot
The which I could not love the less;
So lovely was the loneliness
Of a wild lake, with black rock bound,
And the tall trees that tower'd around.
But when the night had thrown her pall
Upon that spot — as upon all,
And the wind would pass me by
In its stilly melody,
My infant spirit would awake
To the terror of the lone lake.
Yet that terror was not fright —
But a tremulous delight,
And a feeling undefin'd,
Springing from a darken'd mind.
Death was in that poison'd wave
And in its gulf a fitting grave
For him who thence could solace bring
To his dark imagining;
Whose wild'ring thought could even make
An Eden of that dim lake.

[1827]

SONNET — TO SCIENCE

Science! true daughter of Old Time thou art!
  Who alterest all things with thy peering eyes.
Why preyest thou thus upon the poet's heart,
  Vulture, whose wings are dull realities?
How should he love thee? or how deem thee wise,
  Who wouldst not leave him in his wandering
To seek for treasure in the jewelled skies,
  Albeit he soared with an undaunted wing?
Hast thou not dragged Diana from her car?
  And driven the Hamadryad from the wood
To seek a shelter in some happier star?
  Hast thou not torn the Naiad from her flood,
The Elfin from the green grass, and from me
The summer dream beneath the tamarind tree?

[1829–1843]

14

[ALONE]

From childhood's hour I have not been
As others were — I have not seen
As others saw — I could not bring
My passions from a common spring —
From the same source I have not taken
My sorrow — I could not awaken
My heart to joy at the same tone —
And all I lov'd — *I* lov'd alone —
Then — in my childhood — in the dawn
Of a most stormy life — was drawn
From ev'ry depth of good and ill
The mystery which binds me still —
From the torrent, or the fountain —
From the red cliff of the mountain —
From the sun that 'round me roll'd
In its autumn tint of gold —
From the lightning in the sky
As it pass'd me flying by —
From the thunder, and the storm —
And the cloud that took the form
(When the rest of Heaven was blue)
Of a demon in my view —

[1829]

INTRODUCTION

Romance, who loves to nod and sing,
With drowsy head and folded wing,
Among the green leaves as they shake
Far down within some shadowy lake,
To me a painted paroquet
Hath been — a most familiar bird —
Taught me my alphabet to say —
To lisp my very earliest word
While in the wild-wood I did lie
A child — with a most knowing eye.

Succeeding years, too wild for song,
Then roll'd like tropic storms along,
Where, tho' the garish lights that fly
Dying along the troubled sky,
Lay bare, thro' vistas thunder-riven,
The blackness of the general Heaven,
That very blackness yet doth fling
Light on the lightning's silver wing.

For, being an idle boy lang syne,
Who read Anacreon, and drank wine,
I early found Anacreon rhymes
Were almost passionate sometimes —
And by strange alchemy of brain
His pleasures always turn'd to pain —
His naivete to wild desire —
His wit to love — his wine to fire —

And so, being young and dipt in folly
I fell in love with melancholy,
And used to throw my earthly rest
And quiet all away in jest —
I could not love except where Death
Was mingling his with Beauty's breath —
Or Hymen, Time, and Destiny
Were stalking between her and me.

O, then the eternal Condor years
So shook the very Heavens on high,
With tumult as they thunder'd by;
I had no time for idle cares,
Thro' gazing on the unquiet sky!
Or if an hour with calmer wing
Its down did on my spirit fling,
That little hour with lyre and rhyme
To while away — forbidden thing!
My heart half fear'd to be a crime
Unless it trembled with the string.

But *now* my soul hath too much room —
Gone are the glory and the gloom —
The black hath mellow'd into grey,
And all the fires are fading away.

My draught of passion hath been deep —
I revell'd, and I now would sleep —
And after-drunkenness of soul
Succeeds the glories of the bowl —

An idle longing night and day
To dream my very life away.

But dreams — of those who dream as I,
Aspiringly, are damned, and die:
Yet should I swear I mean alone,
By notes so very shrilly blown,
To break upon Time's monotone,
While yet my vapid joy and grief
Are tintless of the yellow leaf —
Why not an imp the greybeard hath,
Will shake his shadow in my path —
And even the greybeard will o'erlook
Connivingly my dreaming-book.

[1829–1831]

TO HELEN

Helen, thy beauty is to me
  Like those Nicéan barks of yore,
That gently, o'er a perfumed sea,
  The weary, way-worn wanderer bore
  To his own native shore.

On desperate seas long wont to roam,
  Thy hyacinth hair, thy classic face,
Thy Naiad airs have brought me home
  To the glory that was Greece,
And the grandeur that was Rome.

Lo! in yon brilliant window-niche
  How statue-like I see thee stand,
  The agate lamp within thy hand!
Ah, Psyche, from the regions which
  Are Holy-Land!

[1831–1843]

ISRAFEL

And the angel Israfel, whose heart-strings are a lute,
and who has the sweetest voice of all God's creatures.
—KORAN.

In Heaven a spirit doth dwell
  "Whose heart-strings are a lute;"
None sing so wildly well
As the angel Israfel,
And the giddy stars (so legends tell)
Ceasing their hymns, attend the spell
  Of his voice, all mute.

Tottering above
  In her highest noon,
  The enamoured moon
Blushes with love,
  While, to listen, the red levin
  (With the rapid Pleiads, even,
  Which were seven,)
  Pauses in Heaven.

And they say (the starry choir
  And the other listening things)
That Israfeli's fire
Is owing to that lyre
  By which he sits and sings —
The trembling living wire
Of those unusual strings.

But the skies that angel trod,
    Where deep thoughts are a duty —
Where Love's a grown-up God —
    Where the Houri glances are
Imbued with all the beauty
    Which we worship in a star.

Therefore, thou art not wrong,
    Israfeli, who despisest
An unimpassioned song;
To thee the laurels belong,
    Best bard, because the wisest!
Merrily live, and long!

The ecstasies above
    With thy burning measures suit —
Thy grief, thy joy, thy hate, thy love,
    With the fervour of thy lute —
    Well may the stars be mute!

Yes, Heaven is thine; but this
    Is a world of sweets and sours;
    Our flowers are merely — flowers,
And the shadow of thy perfect bliss
    Is the sunshine of ours.

If I could dwell
Where Israfel
    Hath dwelt, and he where I,
He might not sing so wildly well

A mortal melody,
While a bolder note than this might swell
From my lyre within the sky.

[1831–1845]

THE VALLEY OF UNREST

Once it smiled a silent dell
Where the people did not dwell;
They had gone unto the wars,
Trusting to the mild-eyed stars,
Nightly, from their azure towers,
To keep watch above the flowers,
In the midst of which all day
The red sun-light lazily lay.
Now each visiter shall confess
The sad valley's restlessness.
Nothing there is motionless.
Nothing save the airs that brood
Over the magic solitude.
Ah, by no wind are stirred those trees
That palpitate like the chill seas
Around the misty Hebrides!
Ah, by no wind those clouds are driven
That rustle through the unquiet Heaven
Uneasily, from morn till even,
Over the violets there that lie
In myriad types of the human eye —
Over the lilies there that wave
And weep above a nameless grave!
They wave: — from out their fragrant tops
Eternal dews come down in drops.
They weep: — from off their delicate stems
Perennial tears descend in gems.

[1831–1845]

THE CITY IN THE SEA

Lo! Death has reared himself a throne
In a strange city lying alone
Far down within the dim West,
Where the good and the bad and the worst and
    the best
Have gone to their eternal rest.
There shrines and palaces and towers
(Time-eaten towers that tremble not!)
Resemble nothing that is ours.
Around, by lifting winds forgot,
Resignedly beneath the sky
The melancholy waters lie.

No rays from the holy heaven come down
On the long night-time of that town;
But light from out the lurid sea
Streams up the turrets silently —
Gleams up the pinnacles far and free
Up domes — up spires — up kingly halls —
Up fanes — up Babylon-like walls —
Up shadowy long-forgotten bowers
Of sculptured ivy and stone flowers —
Up many and many a marvellous shrine
Whose wreathéd friezes intertwine
The viol, the violet, and the vine.

Resignedly beneath the sky
The melancholy waters lie.
So blend the turrets and shadows there

That all seem pendulous in air,
While from a proud tower in the town
Death looks gigantically down.

There open fanes and gaping graves
Yawn level with the luminous waves;
But not the riches there that lie
In each idol's diamond eye —
Not the gaily-jewelled dead
Tempt the waters from their bed;
For no ripples curl, alas!
Along that wilderness of glass —
No swellings tell that winds may be
Upon some far-off happier sea —
No heavings hint that winds have been
On seas less hideously serene.

But lo, a stir is in the air!
The wave — there is a movement there!
As if the towers had thrust aside,
In slightly sinking, the dull tide —
As if their tops had feebly given
A void within the filmy Heaven.
The waves have now a redder glow —
The hours are breathing faint and low —
And when, amid no earthly moans,
Down, down that town shall settle hence,
Hell, rising from a thousand thrones,
Shall do it reverence.

[1831–1845]

TO ONE IN PARADISE

Thou wast that all to me, love,
  For which my soul did pine —
A green isle in the sea, love,
  A fountain and a shrine,
All wreathed with fairy fruits and flowers,
  And all the flowers were mine.

Ah, dream too bright to last!
  Ah, starry Hope! that didst arise
But to be overcast!
  A voice from out the Future cries,
"On! on!" — but o'er the Past
  (Dim gulf!) my spirit hovering lies
Mute, motionless, aghast!

For, alas! alas! with me
  The light of Life is o'er!
No more — no more — no more —
(Such language holds the solemn sea
  To the sands upon the shore)
Shall bloom the thunder-blasted tree,
  Or the stricken eagle soar!

And all my days are trances,
  And all my nightly dreams
Are where thy grey eye glances,
  And where thy footstep gleams —
In what ethereal dances,
By what eternal streams.

[1833–1849]

THE COLISEUM

Type of the antique Rome! Rich reliquary
Of lofty contemplation left to Time
By buried centuries of pomp and power!
At length — at length — after so many days
Of weary pilgrimage and burning thirst,
(Thirst for the springs of lore that in thee lie,)
I kneel, an altered and an humble man,
Amid thy shadows, and so drink within
My very soul thy grandeur, gloom and glory!

Vastness! and Age! and Memories of Eld!
Silence! and Desolation! and dim Night!
I feel ye now — I feel ye in your strength —
O spells more sure than e'er Judæan king
Taught in the gardens of Gethsemane!
O charms more potent than the rapt Chaldee
Ever drew down from out the quiet stars!

Here, where a hero fell, a column falls!
Here, where the mimic eagle glared in gold,
A midnight vigil holds the swarthy bat!
Here, where the dames of Rome their gilded
    hair
Waved to the wind, now wave the reed and
    thistle!
Here, where on golden throne the monarch
    lolled,
Glides, spectre-like, unto his marble home,
Lit by the wan light of the hornéd moon,

27

The swift and silent lizard of the stones!

But stay! these walls — these ivy-clad
    arcades —
These mouldering plinths — these sad and
    blackened shafts —
These vague entablatures — this crumbling
    frieze —
These shattered cornices — this wreck — this
    ruin —
These stones — alas! these gray stones — are
    they all —
All of the famed, and the colossal left
By the corrosive Hours to Fate and me?

"Not all" — the Echoes answer me — "not all!
"Prophetic sounds and loud, arise forever
"From us, and from all Ruin, unto the wise,
"As melody from Memnon to the Sun.
"We rule the hearts of mightiest men — we rule
"With a despotic sway all giant minds.
"We are not impotent — we pallid stones.
"Not all our power is gone — not all our fame —
"Not all the magic of our high renown —
"Not all the wonder that encircles us —
"Not all the mysteries that in us lie —
"Not all the memories that hang upon
"And cling around about us as a garment,
"Clothing us in a robe of more than glory."

[1833–1843]

THE HAUNTED PALACE

In the greenest of our valleys
  By good angels tenanted,
Once a fair and stately palace —
  Radiant palace — reared its head.
In the monarch Thought's dominion —
  It stood there!
Never seraph spread a pinion
  Over fabric half so fair!

Banners yellow, glorious, golden,
  On its roof did float and flow —
(This — all this — was in the olden
  Time long ago)
And every gentle air that dallied,
  In that sweet day,
Along the ramparts plumed and pallid,
  A wingéd odor went away.

Wanderers in that happy valley,
  Through two luminous windows, saw
Spirits moving musically,
  To a lute's well-tunéd law,
Round about a throne where, sitting,
  Porphyrogene,
In state his glory well befitting
  The ruler of the realm was seen.

And all with pearl and ruby glowing
  Was the fair palace door,

29

Through which came flowing, flowing, flowing,
 And sparkling evermore,
A troop of Echoes whose sweet duty
 Was but to sing,
In voices of surpassing beauty,
 The wit and wisdom of their king.

But evil things, in robes of sorrow,
 Assailed the monarch's high estate.
(Ah, let us mourn! — for never morrow
 Shall dawn upon him, desolate!)
And round about his home the glory
 That blushed and bloomed,
Is but a dim-remembered story
 Of the old-time entombed.

And travelers, now, within that valley,
 Through the encrimsoned windows see
Vast forms that move fantastically
 To a discordant melody,
While, like a ghastly rapid river,
 Through the pale door
A hideous throng rush out forever
 And laugh — but smile no more.

[1838–1848]

30

THE CONQUEROR WORM

Lo! 'tis a gala night
  Within the lonesome latter years!
An angel throng, bewinged, bedight
  In veils, and drowned in tears,
Sit in a theatre, to see
  A play of hopes and fears,
While the orchestra breathes fitfully
  The music of the spheres.

Mimes, in the form of God on high,
  Mutter and mumble low,
And hither and thither fly —
  Mere puppets they, who come and go
At bidding of vast formless things
  That shift the scenery to and fro,
Flapping from out their Condor wings
  Invisible Wo!

That motley drama — oh, be sure
  It shall not be forgot!
With its Phantom chased for evermore,
  By a crowd that seize it not,
Through a circle that ever returneth in
  To the self-same spot,
And much of Madness, and more of Sin,
  And Horror the soul of the plot.

But see, amid the mimic rout
  A crawling shape intrude!

A blood-red thing that writhes from out
  The scenic solitude!
It writhes! — it writhes! — with mortal pangs
  The mimes become its food,
And seraphs sob at vermin fangs
  In human gore imbued.

Out — out are the lights — out all!
  And, over each quivering form,
The curtain, a funeral pall,
  Comes down with the rush of a storm,
While the angels, all pallid and wan,
  Uprising, unveiling, affirm
That the play is the tragedy, "Man,"
  And its hero the Conqueror Worm.

[1842–1849]

DREAM-LAND

By a route obscure and lonely,
Haunted by ill angels only,
Where an Eidolon, named Night,
On a black throne reigns upright,
I have reached these lands but newly
From an ultimate dim Thule —
From a wild weird clime that lieth, sublime,
      Out of Space — out of Time.

Bottomless vales and boundless floods,
And chasms, and caves, and Titan woods,
With forms that no man can discover
For the dews that drip all over;
Mountains toppling evermore
Into seas without a shore;
Seas that restlessly aspire,
Surging, unto skies of fire;
Lakes that endlessly outspread
Their lone waters — lone and dead, —
Their still waters — still and chilly
With the snows of the lolling lily.

By the lakes that thus outspread
Their lone waters, lone and dead, —
Their sad waters, sad and chilly
With the snows of the lolling lily, —
By the mountains — near the river
Murmuring lowly, murmuring ever, —
By the grey woods, — by the swamp
Where the toad and the newt encamp, —

By the dismal tarns and pools
     Where dwell the Ghouls, —
By each spot the most unholy —
In each nook most melancholy, —
There the traveller meets aghast
Sheeted Memories of the Past —
Shrouded forms that start and sigh
As they pass the wanderer by —
White-robed forms of friends long given,
In agony, to the Earth — and Heaven.

For the heart whose woes are legion
'Tis a peaceful, soothing region —
For the spirit that walks in shadow
O! it is an Eldorado!
But the traveller, travelling through it,
May not — dare not openly view it;
Never its mysteries are exposed
To the weak human eye unclosed;
So wills its King, who hath forbid
The uplifting of the fringed lid;
And thus the sad Soul that here passes
Beholds it but through darkened glasses.

By a route obscure and lonely,
Haunted by ill angels only,
Where an Eidolon, named NIGHT,
On a black throne reigns upright,
I have wandered home but newly
From this ultimate dim Thule.

[1844–1849]

EULALIE

I dwelt alone
  In a world of moan,
And my soul was a stagnant tide
Till the fair and gentle Eulalie became my
  blushing bride —
Till the yellow-haired young Eulalie became my
  smiling bride.

  Ah, less, less bright
  The stars of the night
Than the eyes of the radiant girl,
    And never a flake
    That the vapor can make
With the moon-tints of purple and pearl
Can vie with the modest Eulalie's most
  unregarded curl —
Can compare with the bright-eyed Eulalie's
  most humble and careless curl.

  Now Doubt — now Pain
  Come never again,
For her soul gives me sigh for sigh
    And all day long
    Shines bright and strong
Astarté within the sky,
While ever to her dear Eulalie upturns her
  matron eye —
While ever to her young Eulalie upturns her
  violet eye.

[1844–1845]

THE RAVEN

Once upon a midnight dreary, while I pondered,
    weak and weary,
Over many a quaint and curious volume of
    forgotten lore —
While I nodded, nearly napping, suddenly there
    came a tapping,
As of some one gently rapping, rapping at my
    chamber door —
" 'Tis some visiter," I muttered, "tapping at my
    chamber door —
        Only this and nothing more."

Ah, distinctly I remember it was in the bleak
    December;
And each separate dying ember wrought its
    ghost upon the floor.
Eagerly I wished the morrow; — vainly I had
    sought to borrow
From my books surcease of sorrow — sorrow for
    the lost Lenore —
For the rare and radiant maiden whom the
    angels name Lenore —
        Nameless *here* for evermore.

And the silken, sad, uncertain rustling of each
    purple curtain
Thrilled me — filled me with fantastic terrors
    never felt before;

So that now, to still the beating of my heart, I
   stood repeating
" 'Tis some visiter entreating entrance at my
   chamber door —
Some late visiter entreating entrance at my
   chamber door; —
      This it is and nothing more."

Presently my soul grew stronger; hesitating
   then no longer,
"Sir," said I, "or Madam, truly your forgiveness
   I implore;
But the fact is I was napping, and so gently you
   came rapping,
And so faintly you came tapping, tapping at my
   chamber door,
That I scarce was sure I heard you" — here I
   opened wide the door; ———
      Darkness there and nothing more.

Deep into that darkness peering, long I stood
   there wondering, fearing,
Doubting, dreaming dreams no mortal ever
   dared to dream before;
But the silence was unbroken, and the stillness
   gave no token,
And the only word there spoken was the
   whispered word, "Lenore?"
This I whispered, and an echo murmured back
   the word, "Lenore!"
      Merely this and nothing more.

Back into the chamber turning, all my soul
  within me burning,
Soon again I heard a tapping somewhat louder
  than before.
"Surely," said I, "surely that is something at my
  window lattice;
Let me see, then, what thereat is, and this
  mystery explore —
Let my heart be still a moment and this
  mystery explore; —
          'Tis the wind and nothing more!"

Open here I flung the shutter, when, with many
  a flirt and flutter,
In there stepped a stately Raven of the saintly
  days of yore;
Not the least obeisance made he; not a minute
  stopped or stayed he;
But, with mien of lord or lady, perched above
  my chamber door —
Perched upon a bust of Pallas just above my
  chamber door —
          Perched, and sat, and nothing more.

Then this ebony bird beguiling my sad fancy
  into smiling,
By the grave and stern decorum of the
  countenance it wore,
"Though thy crest be shorn and shaven, thou," I
  said, "art sure no craven,
Ghastly grim and ancient Raven wandering

from the Nightly shore —
Tell me what thy lordly name is on the Night's
Plutonian shore!"
    Quoth the Raven "Nevermore."

Much I marvelled this ungainly fowl to hear
discourse so plainly.
Though its answer little meaning — little
relevancy bore;
For we cannot help agreeing that no living
human being
Ever yet was blessed with seeing bird above his
chamber door —
Bird or beast upon the sculptured bust above
his chamber door,
    With such name as "Nevermore."

But the Raven, sitting lonely on the placid bust,
spoke only
That one word, as if his soul in that one word
he did outpour.
Nothing farther then he uttered — not a feather
then he fluttered —
Till I scarcely more than muttered "Other
friends have flown before —
On the morrow *he* will leave me, as my Hopes
have flown before."
    Then the bird said "Nevermore."

Startled at the stillness broken by reply so aptly
spoken,

"Doubtless," said I, "what it utters is its only
   stock and store
Caught from some unhappy master whom
   unmerciful Disaster
Followed fast and followed faster till his songs
   one burden bore —
Till the dirges of his Hope that melancholy
   burden bore
      Of 'Never — nevermore.' "

But the Raven still beguiling my sad fancy into
   smiling,
Straight I wheeled a cushioned seat in front of
   bird, and bust and door;
Then, upon the velvet sinking, I betook myself
   to linking
Fancy unto fancy, thinking what this ominous
   bird of yore —
What this grim, ungainly, ghastly, gaunt, and
   ominous bird of yore
      Meant in croaking "Nevermore."

This I sat engaged in guessing, but no syllable
   expressing
To the fowl whose fiery eyes now burned into
   my bosom's core;
This and more I sat divining, with my head at
   ease reclining
On the cushion's velvet lining that the lamp-
   light gloated o'er,

But whose velvet-violet lining with the lamp-
  light gloating o'er,
      She shall press, ah, nevermore!

Then, methought, the air grew denser,
  perfumed from an unseen censer
Swung by seraphim whose foot-falls tinkled on
  the tufted floor.
"Wretch," I cried, "thy God hath lent thee — by
  these angels he hath sent thee
Respite — respite and nepenthe from thy
  memories of Lenore;
Quaff, oh quaff this kind nepenthe and forget
  this lost Lenore!"
      Quoth the Raven "Nevermore."

"Prophet!" said I, "thing of evil! — prophet still,
  if bird or devil! —
Whether Tempter sent, or whether tempest
  tossed thee here ashore,
Desolate yet all undaunted, on this desert land
  enchanted —
On this home by Horror haunted — tell me
  truly, I implore —
Is there — *is* there balm in Gilead? — tell me —
  tell me, I implore!"
      Quoth the Raven "Nevermore."

"Prophet!" said I, "thing of evil! — prophet still,
  if bird or devil!

By that Heaven that bends above us — by that
   God we both adore —
Tell this soul with sorrow laden if, within the
   distant Aidenn,
It shall clasp a sainted maiden whom the angels
   name Lenore —
Clasp a rare and radiant maiden whom the
   angels name Lenore."
        Quoth the Raven "Nevermore."

"Be that word our sign of parting, bird or fiend!"
   I shrieked, upstarting —
"Get thee back into the tempest and the Night's
   Plutonian shore!
Leave no black plume as a token of that lie thy
   soul hath spoken!
Leave my loneliness unbroken! — quit the bust
   above my door!
Take thy beak from out my heart, and take thy
   form from off my door!"
        Quoth the Raven "Nevermore."

And the Raven, never flitting, still is sitting,
   still is sitting
On the pallid bust of Pallas just above my
   chamber door;
And his eyes have all the seeming of a demon's
   that is dreaming,
And the lamp-light o'er him streaming throws
   his shadow on the floor;

And my soul from out that shadow that lies
  floating on the floor
        Shall be lifted — nevermore!

[1844–1849]

[''DEEP IN EARTH'']

Deep in earth my love is lying
And I must weep alone.

[1847]

TO M.L.S——

Of all who hail thy presence as the morning —
Of all to whom thine absence is the night —
The blotting utterly from out high heaven
The sacred sun — of all who, weeping, bless
   thee
Hourly for hope — for life — ah! above all,
For the resurrection of deep-buried faith
In Truth — in Virtue — in Humanity —
Of all who, on Despair's unhallowed bed
Lying down to die, have suddenly arisen
At thy soft-murmured words, "Let there be
   light!"
At the soft-murmured words that were fulfilled
In the seraphic glancing of thine eyes —
Of all who owe thee most — whose gratitude
Nearest resembles worship — oh, remember
The truest — the most fervently devoted,
And think that these weak lines are written by
   him —
By him who, as he pens them, thrills to think
His spirit is communing with an angel's.

[1847]

45

ULALUME — A BALLAD

The skies they were ashen and sober;
   The leaves they were crispéd and sere —
   The leaves they were withering and sere:
It was night, in the lonesome October
   Of my most immemorial year:
It was hard by the dim lake of Auber,
   In the misty mid region of Weir: —
It was down by the dank tarn of Auber,
   In the ghoul-haunted woodland of Weir.

Here once, through an alley Titanic,
   Of cypress, I roamed with my Soul —
   Of cypress, with Psyche, my Soul.
These were days when my heart was volcanic
   As the scoriac rivers that roll —
   As the lavas that restlessly roll
Their sulphurous currents down Yaanek,
   In the ultimate climes of the Pole —
That groan as they roll down Mount Yaanek,
   In the realms of the Boreal Pole.

Our talk had been serious and sober,
   But our thoughts they were palsied and sere —
   Our memories were treacherous and sere;
For we knew not the month was October,
   And we marked not the night of the year —
   (Ah, night of all nights in the year!)
We noted not the dim lake of Auber,
   (Though once we had journeyed down here)

We remembered not the dank tarn of Auber,
  Nor the ghoul-haunted woodland of Weir.

And now, as the night was senescent,
  And star-dials pointed to morn —
  As the star-dials hinted of morn —
At the end of our path a liquescent
  And nebulous lustre was born,
Out of which a miraculous crescent
  Arose with a duplicate horn —
Astarte's bediamonded crescent,
  Distinct with its duplicate horn.

And I said — "She is warmer than Dian;
  She rolls through an ether of sighs —
  She revels in a region of sighs.
She has seen that the tears are not dry on
  These cheeks where the worm never dies,
And has come past the stars of the Lion,
  To point us the path to the skies —
  To the Lethean peace of the skies —
Come up, in despite of the Lion,
  To shine on us with her bright eyes —
Come up, through the lair of the Lion,
  With love in her luminous eyes."

But Psyche, uplifting her finger,
  Said — "Sadly this star I mistrust —
  Her pallor I strangely mistrust —
Ah, hasten! — ah, let us not linger!
  Ah, fly! — let us fly! — for we must."

47

In terror she spoke; letting sink her
  Wings till they trailed in the dust —
In agony sobbed; letting sink her
  Plumes till they trailed in the dust —
  Till they sorrowfully trailed in the dust.

I replied — "This is nothing but dreaming.
  Let us on, by this tremulous light!
  Let us bathe in this crystalline light!
Its Sibyllic splendor is beaming
  With Hope and in Beauty to-night —
  See! — it flickers up the sky through the night!
Ah, we safely may trust to its gleaming
  And be sure it will lead us aright —
We surely may trust to a gleaming
    That cannot but guide us aright
Since it flickers up to Heaven through the
  night."

Thus I pacified Psyche and kissed her,
  And tempted her out of her gloom —
  And conquered her scruples and gloom;
And we passed to the end of the vista —
  But were stopped by the door of a tomb —
  By the door of a legended tomb: —
And I said — "What is written, sweet sister,
  On the door of this legended tomb?"
  She replied — "Ulalume — Ulalume! —
  'T is the vault of thy lost Ulalume!"

Then my heart it grew ashen and sober

As the leaves that were crispéd and sere —
As the leaves that were withering and sere —
And I cried — "It was surely October,
  On *this* very night of last year,
  That I journeyed — I journeyed down here! —
  That I brought a dread burden down here —
  On this night, of all nights in the year,
  Ah, what demon hath tempted me here?
Well I know, now, this dim lake of Auber —
  This misty mid region of Weir: —
Well I know, now, this dank tarn of Auber —
  This ghoul-haunted woodland of Weir."

Said we, then — the two, then — "Ah, can it
  Have been that the woodlandish ghouls —
  The pitiful, the merciful ghouls,
To bar up our way and to ban it
  From the secret that lies in these wolds —
  From the thing that lies hidden in these
  wolds —
Have drawn up the spectre of a planet
  From the limbo of lunary souls —
This sinfully scintillant planet
  From the Hell of the planetary souls?"

                                   [1847–1849]

THE BELLS

1.

Hear the sledges with the bells —
Silver bells!
What a world of merriment their melody foretells!
How they tinkle, tinkle, tinkle,
In the icy air of night!
While the stars that oversprinkle
All the Heavens, seem to twinkle
With a crystalline delight;
Keeping time, time, time,
In a sort of Runic rhyme,
To the tintinabulation that so musically wells
From the bells, bells, bells, bells,
Bells, bells, bells —
From the jingling and the tinkling of the bells.

2.

Hear the mellow wedding bells —
Golden bells!
What a world of happiness their harmony foretells!
Through the balmy air of night
How they ring out their delight! —
From the molten-golden notes
And all in tune,
What a liquid ditty floats
To the turtle-dove that listens while she gloats
On the moon!
Oh, from out the sounding cells
What a gush of euphony voluminously wells!

How it swells!
How it dwells
On the Future! — how it tells
Of the rapture that impels
To the swinging and the ringing
Of the bells, bells, bells! —
Of the bells, bells, bells, bells,
Bells, bells, bells —
To the rhyming and the chiming of the bells!

3.

Hear the loud alarum bells —
Brazen bells!
What tale of terror, now, their turbulency tells!
In the startled ear of Night
How they scream out their affright!
Too much horrified to speak,
They can only shriek, shriek,
Out of tune,
In a clamorous appealing to the mercy of the fire —
In a mad expostulation with the deaf and frantic fire,
Leaping higher, higher, higher,
With a desperate desire
And a resolute endeavor
Now — now to sit, or never,
By the side of the pale-faced moon.
Oh, the bells, bells, bells!
What a tale their terror tells
Of despair!
How they clang and clash and roar!
What a horror they outpour

In the bosom of the palpitating air!
　　Yet the ear, it fully knows,
　　　By the twanging
　　　And the clanging,
　　How the danger ebbs and flows: —
　　Yes, the ear distinctly tells,
　　　In the jangling
　　　And the wrangling,
　　How the danger sinks and swells,
By the sinking or the swelling in the anger of the bells —
　　　Of the bells —
　Of the bells, bells, bells, bells,
　　　Bells, bells, bells —
　　In the clamor and the clangor of the bells.

4.

　　Hear the tolling of the bells —
　　　Iron bells!
What a world of solemn thought their monody compels!
　　In the silence of the night
　　How we shiver with affright
　At the melancholy meaning of the tone!
　　For every sound that floats
　　From the rust within their throats
　　　Is a groan.
　　And the people — ah, the people
　　They that dwell up in the steeple
　　　All alone,
　And who, tolling, tolling, tolling,
　　In that muffled monotone,
　Feel a glory in so rolling

On the human heart a stone —
They are neither man nor woman —
They are neither brute nor human,
    They are Ghouls: —
And their king it is who tolls: —
And he rolls, rolls, rolls, rolls
    A Pæan from the bells!
And his merry bosom swells
    With the Pæan of the bells!
And he dances and he yells;
Keeping time, time, time,
In a sort of Runic rhyme,
    To the Pæan of the bells —
      Of the bells: —
Keeping time, time, time,
In a sort of Runic rhyme,
    To the throbbing of the bells —
Of the bells, bells, bells —
    To the sobbing of the bells: —
Keeping time, time, time,
    As he knells, knells, knells,
In a happy Runic rhyme,
    To the rolling of the bells —
Of the bells, bells, bells: —
    To the tolling of the bells —
Of the bells, bells, bells, bells,
    Bells, bells, bells —
To the moaning and the groaning of the bells.

[July 1849]

TO HELEN [WHITMAN]

I saw thee once — once only — years ago:
I must not say *how* many — but *not* many.
It was a July midnight; and from out
A full-orbed moon, that, like thine own soul, soaring,
Sought a precipitate pathway up through heaven,
There fell a silvery-silken veil of light,
With quietude, and sultriness, and slumber,
Upon the upturn'd faces of a thousand
Roses that grew in an enchanted garden,
Where no wind dared to stir, unless on tiptoe —
Fell on the upturn'd faces of these roses
That gave out, in return for the love-light,
Their odorous souls in an ecstatic death —
Fell on the upturn'd faces of these roses
That smiled and died in this parterre, enchanted
By thee, and by the poetry of thy presence.

Clad all in white, upon a violet bank
I saw thee half reclining; while the moon
Fell on the upturn'd faces of the roses,
And on thine own, upturn'd — alas, in sorrow!

Was it not Fate, that, on this July midnight —
Was it not Fate, (whose name is also Sorrow,)
That bade me pause before that garden-gate,

To breathe the incense of those slumbering
   roses?
No footstep stirred: the hated world all slept,
Save only thee and me. (Oh, Heaven! — oh,
   God!
How my heart beats in coupling those two
   words!)
Save only thee and me. I paused — I looked —
And in an instant all things disappeared.
(Ah, bear in mind this garden was enchanted!)
The pearly lustre of the moon went out:
The mossy banks and the meandering paths,
The happy flowers and the repining trees,
Were seen no more: the very roses' odors
Died in the arms of the adoring airs.
All — all expired save thee — save less than
   thou:
Save only the divine light in thine eyes —
Save but the soul in thine uplifted eyes.
I saw but them — they were the world to me.
I saw but them — saw only them for hours —
Saw only them until the moon went down.
What wild heart-histories seemed to lie
   enwritten
Upon those crystalline, celestial spheres!
How dark a wo! yet how sublime a hope!
How silently serene a sea of pride!
How daring an ambition! yet how deep —
How fathomless a capacity for love!
But now, at length, dear Dian sank from sight,

Into a western couch of thunder-cloud;
And thou, a ghost, amid the entombing trees
Didst glide away. *Only thine eyes remained.*
They *would not* go — they never yet have gone.
Lighting my lonely pathway home that night,
They have not left me (as my hopes have) since.
They follow me — they lead me through the
    years.
They are my ministers — yet I their slave.
Their office is to illumine and enkindle —
My duty, *to be saved* by their bright light,
And purified in their electric fire,
And sanctified in their elysian fire.
They fill my soul with Beauty (which is Hope,)
And are far up in Heaven — the stars I kneel to
In the sad, silent watches of my night;
While even in the meridian glare of day
I see them still — two sweetly scintillant
Venuses, unextinguished by the sun!

[1848–1849]

56

A DREAM WITHIN A DREAM

Take this kiss upon the brow!
And, in parting from you now,
Thus much let me avow —
You are not wrong, who deem
That my days have been a dream;
Yet if hope has flown away
In a night, or in a day,
In a vision, or in none,
Is it therefore the less *gone*?
All that we see or seem
Is but a dream within a dream.

I stand amid the roar
Of a surf-tormented shore,
And I hold within my hand
Grains of the golden sand —
How few! yet how they creep
Through my fingers to the deep,
While I weep — while I weep!
O God! can I not grasp
Them with a tighter clasp?
O God! can I not save
One from the pitiless wave?
Is *all* that we see or seem
But a dream within a dream?

[1849]

FOR ANNIE

Thank Heaven! the crisis —
  The danger is past,
And the lingering illness
  Is over at last —
And the fever called "Living"
  Is conquered at last.

Sadly, I know
  I am shorn of my strength,
And no muscle I move
  As I lie at full length —
But no matter! — I feel
  I am better at length.

And I rest so composedly,
  Now, in my bed,
That any beholder
  Might fancy me dead —
Might start at beholding me,
  Thinking me dead.

The moaning and groaning,
  The sighing and sobbing,
Are quieted now,
  With that horrible throbbing
At heart: — ah, that horrible,
  Horrible throbbing!

The sickness — the nausea —

The pitiless pain —
Have ceased, with the fever
  That maddened my brain —
With the fever called "Living"
  That burned in my brain.

And oh! of all tortures
  That torture the worst
Has abated — the terrible
  Torture of thirst
For the napthaline river
  Of Passion accurst: —
I have drank of a water
  That quenches all thirst —

Of a water that flows,
  With a lullaby sound,
From a spring but a very few
  Feet under ground —
From a cavern not very far
  Down under ground.

And ah! let it never
  Be foolishly said
That my room it is gloomy
  And narrow my bed;
For man never slept
  In a different bed —
And, to *sleep*, you must slumber
  In just such a bed.

My tantalized spirit
   Here blandly reposes,
Forgetting, or never
   Regretting its roses —
Its old agitations
   Of myrtles and roses:

For now, while so quietly
   Lying, it fancies
A holier odor
   About it, of pansies —
A rosemary odor,
   Commingled with pansies —
With rue and the beautiful
   Puritan pansies.

And so it lies happily,
   Bathing in many
A dream of the truth
   And the beauty of Annie —
Drowned in a bath
   Of the tresses of Annie.

She tenderly kissed me,
   She fondly caressed,
And then I fell gently
   To sleep on her breast —
Deeply to sleep
   From the heaven of her breast.

When the light was extinguished,
    She covered me warm,
And she prayed to the angels
    To keep me from harm —
To the queen of the angels
    To shield me from harm.

And I lie so composedly,
    Now, in my bed,
(Knowing her love)
    That you fancy me dead —
And I rest so contentedly,
    Now in my bed,
(With her love at my breast)
    That you fancy me dead —
That you shudder to look at me,
    Thinking me dead: —

But my heart it is brighter
    Than all of the many
Stars in the sky,
    For it sparkles with Annie —
It glows with the light
    Of the love of my Annie —
With the thought of the light
    Of the eyes of my Annie.

[1849]

ELDORADO

Gaily bedight,
  A gallant knight,
In sunshine and in shadow,
  Had journeyed long,
  Singing a song,
In search of Eldorado.

But he grew old —
  This knight so bold —
And o'er his heart a shadow
  Fell, as he found
  No spot of ground
That looked like Eldorado.

And, as his strength
  Failed him at length
He met a pilgrim shadow —
  "Shadow," said he,
  "Where can it be —
This land of Eldorado?"

"Over the Mountains
  Of the Moon,
Down the Valley of the Shadow,
  Ride, boldly ride,"
  The shade replied, —
"If you seek for Eldorado!"

[1849]

TO MY MOTHER

Because I feel that, in the Heavens above,
   The angels, whispering to one another,
Can find, among their burning terms of love,
   None so devotional as that of "Mother,"
Therefore by that dear name I long have called
      you —
   You who are more than mother unto me,
And fill my heart of hearts, where Death
      installed you
   In setting my Virginia's spirit free.
My mother — my own mother, who died early,
   Was but the mother of myself; but you
Are mother to the one I loved so dearly,
   And thus are dearer than the mother I knew
By that infinity with which my wife
   Was dearer to my soul than its soul-life.

[1849]

63

ANNABEL LEE

It was many and many a year ago,
  In a kingdom by the sea,
That a maiden there lived whom you may know
  By the name of Annabel Lee; —
And this maiden she lived with no other
  thought
  Than to love and be loved by me.

I was a child and *she* was a child,
  In this kingdom by the sea;
But we loved with a love that was more than
  love —
  I and my Annabel Lee —
With a love that the wingéd seraphs in Heaven
  Coveted her and me.

And this was the reason that, long ago,
  In this kingdom by the sea,
A wind blew out of a cloud, chilling
  My beautiful Annabel Lee;
So that her high-born kinsmen came
  And bore her away from me,
To shut her up in a sepulchre,
  In this kingdom by the sea.

The angels, not half so happy in Heaven,
  Went envying her and me —
Yes! — that was the reason (as all men know,
  In this kingdom by the sea)

That the wind came out of the cloud by night,
  Chilling and killing my Annabel Lee.

But our love it was stronger by far than the
    love
  Of those who were older than we —
  Of many far wiser than we —
And neither the angels in Heaven above,
  Nor the demons down under the sea,
Can ever dissever my soul from the soul
  Of the beautiful Annabel Lee: —

For the moon never beams, without bringing me
    dreams
  Of the beautiful Annabel Lee;
And the stars never rise, but I feel the bright
    eyes
  Of the beautiful Annabel Lee: —
And so, all the night-tide, I lie down by the side
Of my darling — my darling — my life and my
    bride,
  In her sepulchre there by the sea —
  In her tomb by the sounding sea.

[May 1849]

INDEX OF FIRST LINES

INDEX OF POEMS

FOR FURTHER
INFORMATION

Readers wishing to explore further the writings of Edgar Allan Poe may wish to consult the following editions:

Mabbot, Thomas Ollive, ed. *Collected Works of Edgar Allan Poe.* 3 vols. Cambridge: Harvard University Press, 1969–78.

Pollin, Burton R., ed. *Collected Writings of Edgar Allan Poe.* 4 vols. to date. Boston: Twayne, 1981; New York: Gordian Press, 1985–.

Ostrom, John Ward, ed. *The Letters of Edgar Allan Poe.* rev. ed. 2 vols. New York: Gordian Press, 1966.

Those wishing to learn more about Poe's life may wish to examine the following biographical works:

Allen, Hervey. *Israfel—The Life and Times of Edgar Allan Poe.* New York: Farrar & Rinehart, 1934.

Quinn, Arthur Hobson. *Edgar Allan Poe—A Critical Biography.* New York: D. Appleton-Century, 1941.

Silverman, Kenneth. *Edgar A. Poe—Mourn-ful and Never-ending Remembrance*. New York: HarperCollins, 1991.

Thomas, Dwight, and David K. Jackson. *The Poe Log—A Documentary Life of Edgar Allan Poe 1809–1849*. Boston: G. K. Hall, 1987.

The following periodicals concern Poe's life and writing:

The Poe Messenger (The Poe Museum, 1914–16 East Main Street, Richmond, Virgina 23223).

Poe Studies/Dark Romanticism (Washington State University Press, Pullman, Washington 99164).

Poe Studies Association Newsletter (Poe Studies Association, English Department, Western Oregon State College, Monmouth, Oregon 97361).

The following museums and sites importantly illuminate Poe and his world:

The Poe Museum (1914–16 East Main Street, Richmond, Virginia 23223).

The Poe Cottage (Grand Concourse and Kingsbridge Road, Bronx, New York 10458).

Edgar Allan Poe National Historic Site (532 North 7th Street, Philadelphia, Pennsylvania 19123).

Edgar Allan Poe Room (c/o University Guides Service, The Rotunda, University of Virginia, Charlottesville, Virginia 22903).

Edgar Allan Poe House (203 North Amity Street, Baltimore, Maryland 21223).

Fort Moultrie Visitors Center (1214 Middle Street, Sullivan's Island, South Carolina 29482).

The Casemate Museum (Fort Monroe, Virginia 23651).

The Providence Athenaeum (251 Benefit Street, Providence, Rhode Island 02903).